GLORIA
Children's Books

Nihil Obstat, Arthur J. Scanlan, S.T.D., Censor Liborum
Imprimatur ✠ Francis Cardinal Spellman,
Archbishop of New York
Cum Permissu Superiorum

William J. Hirten Co., Cumberland, RI

GLORIA
Children's Books

THE
OUR FATHER

"Our Prayer to God"

by Daniel A. Lord, S.J.

The Lord's Prayer:
The Our Father

This prayer is the most
important prayer Jesus gave us.
This is the most perfect prayer.
It is the summary
of the whole Gospel.
Jesus says to me,
"Ask and you will receive."
I pray this prayer with my heart
many times a day.

"Christ with the Little Children"

Our Father, who art in Heaven,
Hallowed be thy name;
thy Kingdom come;
Thy will be done on earth
As it is in Heaven.
Give us this day our daily bread.
And forgive us our
trespasses
As we forgive those who
trespass againt us.
And lead us not into
temptation.
But deliver us from evil.
Amen.

Our Father,
who art in Heaven...

God is my Father.
He is everyone's Father.
He says to call Him Abba, Daddy!
He made my body and my soul.
He gave me everything good.
He made me to know Him,
to love Him, and to obey Him.
He wants me to come to
Him some day in Heaven
There I shall be very happy with
Him and the Saints forever.

Hallowed by Thy name...

This means I hope everyone
will love my Father in Heaven.
I want them all to say kind
things about Him
and to praise
His holy Name.
I hope everyone
will know Him.
I hope they will
all love Him as I do.

Thy Kingdom Come...

I am a little Catholic. I love Jesus.
I belong to God's Kingdom.
Besides being patriotic,
I am also a Christian.
I wish everyone was Catholic too.
They would get
so many gifts from God.
They would know so many things
to make them happy.
They would know
that God loves them, too.

13

Thy will be done on earth
as it is in Heaven...

In Heaven everyone does God's will.
That is why everyone
is happy there.
There are Angels
and Saints in Heaven with God.
On earth, lots of people are unhappy.
They do not do what God wants.
They commit sin.
I wish people on earth were like
the happy Saints in Heaven.

15

Give us this day
our daily bread...

My Father in Heaven
gives me everthing I need.
He gives me my food.
He gives me my clothes.
He gives me
the Sacraments of grace.
So I ask Him to keep on
giving me all I need.
I know He will, if I trust in Him.

And forgive us our trespasses...

Trespasses are naughty bad things.
Trespasses are my sins.
Sometimes I am naughty.
Somtimes I do things
that are not nice.
These are sins.
I ask God to forgive my sins, please.
He promises He will,
if I am truly sorry.

As we forgive those who trespass against us.

Sometimes people
are not nice to me.
They hurt my feelings.
They do unkind things to me.
But I will not be angry.
I forgive them.
Then God will forgive me
when I do unkind things to Him.

And lead us not into temptation...

The world is full of dangers.
Sometimes bad people
try to harm us.
They try to make us sin.
The evil spirits hate us too.
We ask our Father
to take care of us.
We say
"Please don't let us fall into sin.
Please don't let us run into danger."

23

But deliver us from evil.

The world is full of sad things, too.
The devil tries
to trick us to do evil.
But, we do not want
to sin and be sad.
We want to be happy.
So we ask God to take care of us.
Little children can be hurt easily.
But we pray to our Father.
He won't let anything hurt us.

Amen.

This is a word
that ends our prayers.
It means:
"Please do this, my Father.
I hope what I ask will take place."
Then I say the "Hail Mary."